What Is an Adverb?

Dearly, Nearly, Insincerely

Adverb: A word that describes when, how, where, how often and how much.

Dearly, Nearly, Insincerely

What Is an Adverb?

by Brian P Cleary

illustrated by Brian Gable

LERNER BOOKS · LONDON · NEW YORK · MINNEAPOLIS

Adverbs tell us
when and how.

Like,
quickly
do your
homework,
now.

4

They often help describe the verbs,

Like, **patiently** plant peas and herbs.

PEAS

Adverbs will frequently
end in 'L-Y',

As in viciously,
ultra-suspiciously sly.

6

Adverbs add character,
sizzle and fizz

To your phrase or your
sentence, whatever it is!

7

Sharply, my dad said to hand him a razor.

Lightly, I asked him, 'Did you see that laser?'

8

Frankly, this hot dog just couldn't be better.

Sheepishly, Fred found he'd ruined his sweater.

If they tell us **how**, they're an 'adVerb of manner',

Like, slowly this summer, my sister got tanner.

'Frequency adverbs' will tell us **how often**,

Like, seldom have I seen a lovelier coffin.

Always eat cookies and never eat pine.

Sometimes I'm nervous, but usually fine.

13

Adverbs can help in explaining how much,

As in, this is extremely delightful to touch.

Or Johnny is somewhat afraid of the spider,

And Mickey has hardly been touching his cider.

They give us a time,
a place and
a number,

Like, yesterday, over there,
I was in slumber.

First, I was tired,

then, I was woozy,

Next, I began feeling sleepy and snoozy.

They modify **adverbs**, like, she sang quite nicely.

Or he speaks so swiftly but **very** precisely.

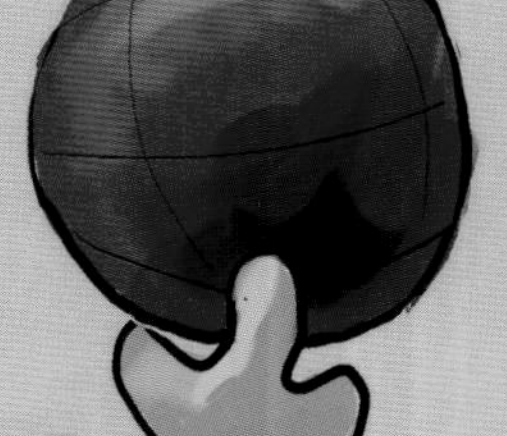

Curiously, furiously,
strikingly strong,

Helplessly lost and
hopelessly wrong.

Adverbs, you'll find,
give the adjectives zip!

As in foolishly frisky

and famously hip —

Bitterly angry, bitingly cold,

Brilliantly burgundy, shockingly old.

The adjective's 'good',
the **adverb** is 'well'.

So now that
you know that,
you're able to tell

That well's how you felt,
and good was your day.

Yes, well is a
very deep subject,
I'd say!

Truly, deeply,
Sadly, badly —

TRULY

DEEPLY

SADLY

BADLY

I tell you these are
adverbs, gladly.

And so are
sleekly and
uniquely,

Bravely,
boldly,

coldly, meekly.

Brightly, slightly, impolitely –

You'd say that these
are **adVerbs**, rightly.

So, what is an **adVerb?**

Do you know?

ABOUT THE AUTHOR & ILLUSTRATOR

BRIAN P CLEARY is the author of the best-selling Words Are CATegorical™ series and the Math Is CATegorical™ series, as well as Peanut Butter and Jellyfishes: A Very Silly Alphabet Book, Rainbow Soup: Adventures in Poetry, and Rhyme & PUNishment: Adventures in Wordplay. Mr Cleary lives in Cleveland, Ohio, USA.

BRIAN GABLE is the illustrator of several Words Are CATegorical™ books, as well as the Math Is CATegorical™ series. Mr Gable also works as a political cartoonist for the Globe and Mail newspaper in Toronto, Canada.

Text copyright © 2003 by Brian P Cleary
Illustrations copyright © 2003 by Lerner Publishing Group, Inc.

First published in the United States of America in 2003

First published in the United Kingdom in 2009 by
Lerner Books,
Dalton House,
60 Windsor Avenue,
London SW19 2RR

Website address: www.lernerbooks.co.uk

This edition was updated and edited for UK publication by Discovery Books Ltd.,
Unit 3, 37 Watling Street, Leintwardine, Shropshire, SY7 0LW

British Library Cataloguing in Publication Data

Cleary, Brian P., 1959-
Nearly, dearly, insincerely : what is an adverb?. – 2nd ed. –
(Words are categorical)
1. English language – Adverb – Juvenile poetry
I. Title
425.7'6

ISBN-13: 978 0 7613 4270 0

Printed in China